Advance Praise

Every seed—each pinprick of promise in this green world—is a masterwork. And this *Seed,* this most recent collection of Janice Gould's poems, is unmistakably the work of a master. Arising from deep wisdom and humility, these lines flower from the poet's body. Clear and potently accessible, her poetry emerges from her spirit-borne vision, a vision wedded to the earth's sensory richness. How closely she looks, how wisely she sees into her own dark and complicated affections. *Seed* is the gift from this master at her work.
—Paulann Petersen, Oregon Poet Laureate Emerita

"To live a peaceful life is no easy thing," writes Janice Gould, and I might add that it's no easy thing to write a deeply satisfying peaceful poem. But *Seed,* as a whole, is a collection of poems that find peace in difficult places. The peace inside longing. The peace inside discrimination. The peace inside confusion, despair, shadow. I love the way Janice Gould blurs the lines between the human and more-than human realms of heart, garden, dream, and animal. I love her attention to slight details. *Seed* is beautiful. Heartbreaking. Strong. Vulnerable. I love this book of love poems, how they invite us, too, into compassion, possibility, attentiveness, and, yes, even peace.
 —Rosemerry Wahtola Trommer, author of *Naked for Tea* and *Even Now*

I have admired Janice Gould's poetry for many years, and now the poems in *Seed* offer me even more to praise. Such lyric simplicity is hard-earned, and comes from a rare depth of experience. The range of approaches and voices that I have always associated with Gould's work recurs in such poems as "Fierce Defense," a bitter monologue of opposition, and "Black Hair," an intimately observed narrative of desire. "I know

nothing about the soul," she writes in another poem, but it is precisely the quality of soul her writing evokes that makes me cherish this book.
—David Mason, author of *The Sound: New and Selected Poems*

Seed will haunt you as it has me—I cannot stop reading it aloud. Like the weeds and roses it invokes, the collection digs in, quietly at first, sending tendrils of images—flowers, morning stars, and green shoots of desire—that remain rooted in the heart long after the last page has closed. Brought to us by the brilliant Janice Gould, author of powerful books like B*eneath My Heart, Doubters and Dreamers,* and most recently, *The Force of Gratitude, Seed* will open you to the sacred of the everyday. In it, Gould writes the ceremony that is our breath, our lives, our loves. For this gift, for these words, for this gorgeous collection, I am thankful.
—Lisa Tatonetti, author of *The Queerness of Native American Literature*

Janice Gould's exquisite collection moves smoothly through love lyrics into narratives that tell stories of struggles as a lesbian in a hostile world. Poems are carefully linked together, leading the reader into a sequence rather than a random collection. The poet experiences life through a natural world that she observes with intimate knowledge and love. Death, the man in black with his face averted, haunts the edges of the poems more and more, as she claims to know nothing about the soul, yet unearths her deepest wisdom about the shared journey towards the home where we will be finally welcomed.
—Judith Barrington, author of *Long Love: New & Selected Poems*

Whether you seek a friend, or The Friend, a mother or The Mother, these poems are the companion you've been waiting for. In here, being a woman whose heart surges with the sweet

music of love for women—and recollecting how difficult that was, as a girl—becomes the difficult and gilded path of finding any human way in the dark. Being a seeker and supplicant on holy earth in New Mexico becomes the state of seeking connection to The Beyond from anywhere. These are redolent poems, aromatherapy for the skittish soul. They literally made me laugh and cry. These are poems to breathe and live.
—Maria Melendez Kelson, author of *Flexible Bones* and *How Long She'll Last in This World*

Books by Janice Gould

Poetry Collections

Beneath My Heart
Firebrand Books, 1990

Earthquake Weather
University of Arizona Press, 1996

Alphabet
May Day Press, 1996

Doubters and Dreamers
University of Arizona Press, 2011

The Force of Gratitude
Headmistress Press, 2017

Seed
Headmistress Press, 2019

Editor

Speak to Me Words: Essays on Contemporary American Indian Poetry
University of Arizona Press, 2003

Seed

Seed

Janice Gould

HEADMISTRESS PRESS

ISBN 978-1-7335345-0-5

Cover photo (photographer unkown): the author's father, Geoffrey
Gould (who became Barbara Bentley in 1990), and the author (Janice
Gould), probably taken around 1955.
Author photo by Pat Musick.
Cover & book design by Mary Meriam.

PUBLISHER
Headmistress Press
60 Shipview Lane
Sequim, WA 98382
Telephone: 917-428-8312
Email: headmistresspress@gmail.com
Website: headmistresspress.blogspot.com

For Mimi,

For my sisters,

And for all my relations

Contents

A Cherokee elder told me, "Look at everything three times. Once with the right eye. Once with the left eye. And once from the corners of the eyes to see the spirit [essence] of what you're looking at."

–Marilou Awiakta
Selu: Seeking the Corn-Mother's Wisdom

A Poem

is about to flower
full force from my abdomen,
my spleen, my wrists,
my ankles. I could feel
the pip of it in last night's dream
that kept threading its way
back to sacred land, where
I found myself in my twenties,
and where, later, you and I
were dream-happy. Our house,
the one that appears in all
the strange locales you and I
dream-inhabit, could be seen
dimly through the pines
on a dry hillside. Our landlady
was there, stooping over her garden.
We are always moving in
or moving away from that
falling-down place made of stone,
or weathered wood, or adobe.
But just passing by our old home
as I did in last night's dream
made me feel excited—yes,
there it is!—and serene,
like seeing an old friend.
And when I woke, I longed
for that familiar dreamscape,
as if it is a real land, as if
that dark earth the landlady turns
with her trowel is scented

with loam, is mapped with leaves
and small roots, as if the wind
blowing dust down the mountain road
is an actual wind, as if a poem
could emerge from a seed.

Seed

For years it remained dormant,
gathering necessity
in the warmth of earth,
accruing strength
within its sturdy pod.
How strange that soil offers itself
as habitat for flowering,
that detritus becomes
nourishment. Rain arrives,
falling in clear drops,
slaking this thirst.
Love starts up silently,
sheathed and verdant,
breaking its way
toward you,
toward light.

Garden

Forgive me, soil, for spading up
unwanted weeds and vines.
Forgive me, ants, for disturbing
your busy endeavors, your industrious
highways. The beloved will walk
here one day, noticing the care
I have given, relishing the tended
and tender growth. Her hand
will reach toward each rose,
her finger will touch the fringe
of each petal. A small wind,
warm and fragrant, will cause her
to turn, to look at me, to moisten
the rose of her lips.

Rose

Little by little the bud forms, protected
in its green cup. Then scarlet, white, or
many-colored, the flower of its body
begins to unfurl helplessly,
its spiral self opening, following
the summons of its nature
or this nurture. I watch the rose
dip to her as she walks by.
Even its thorns caress her,
wanting her touch.

Weed

I am a weed in your perfect garden
hidden behind the rose. I grew
at first unbidden
from a tiny kernal
left here by a sparrow
or a finch. I remained
a mere sprout until I realized
I like sunshine,
fine mulch,
and cool water soaking my roots.
Then I found myself trusting
the sheltering rose, her scent,
her slender stalk,
the vividness of her reds,
the mellowness of her whites.
After that I grew intentionally,
absorbing every drop
of moisture that fell
from her leaves, droplet
by droplet, onto the thirsty
patch of soil that sustains me.
I know you find me coarse
and repulsive, my flower
plain, my leaves
unattractive. I admit
I'm scratchy, whether squat
or gangly, my scent
not sweet, but acrid.
Still, bees come
to my awkward blossom,

and the wind twists me,
just as it bends the rose.
Creator made me for some
unstated purpose, perhaps
to annoy and displease you,
to disrupt your fundamental beliefs
about order and meaning.
Or to offer you another way
to see beauty.

River

How strong this channel has become,
the river widening at the bend,
creating shoals and back currents,
where chilly water will be warmed
by sun, and willows sprout
along the graveled shore. I hear
bees among the blackberries,
can smell their prickly fragrance,
and some days I think I see her
on the other side, near the edge,
surveying the wild current, noticing
how the wind rips along the surface of water.
She watches all that shining where forces collide—
otherwise known as my heart.

Migration

Miles spread out before us, vast
and lonely. Fleeing, we traveled
a familiar trail, crossing high plateaus,
stark and numbing as history.
Too worn down to celebrate
our freedom, we vanished quietly
like Indians, making our way
north and west, rattling
down the highway
in an outsized truck.
Far off the ocean churned
against the gravelly shore,
but first there were rivers to follow,
long stretches of wheat fields,
forests, cliffs of black lava.
Days later we stood in a city of bridges
watching swirls of water darken
as the sun crested the wooded hills.
Not certain what lay before us,
weary and stunned, we were thankful
for friends who offered a place to live.
Then the rain came, cold and clean,
eroding the worst memories,
creating a new habitat of vine maple,
hemlock, blackberry and salal.
Under the cabin's eaves
we listened to wet staccato
on the metal roof, the rush of wind.
We huddled near the wood stove,
sipped tea, stoked the fire

with dry cedar. Our thoughts
were not yet complete, but
restoration seemed possible.
Mist rose from the meadow,
the creek tumbled down its narrow bed,
loosening stones. Ravens called,
moles burrowed, ferns unfurled
their welcoming fronds.
We shivered, relieved,
and sometimes wept
as we remade our lives.

Rain

We love female rain, my beloved and I.
In our small shelter beneath the trees
we live quietly, while outside
an earthly mist arises
to meet the cloud of droplets
that spatter the metal roof
and drench ferns and blackberries,
hemlock and trillium
over sodden hours. After the storm,
when we venture outdoors, I whisper,
Lift your face, and she does, smiling at the sky,
chin tilted heavenward. A few angels
have gathered on the wooden deck,
gossamer vestments wet and
sparkling. They copy her exactly.

Dream

In the dream I searched for you, roaming
upstairs hallways in that elegant house
built in another era. I noticed the furnishings—
upholstered straight-backed chairs,
a glass-topped table, a chandelier,
French doors. *If someone sees me,*
I thought, *they will take me for a thief.*
I quickly left. But you had been here,
I could sense that, and a great sadness
filled me. Outside, winter rain drifted
over the west hills, the drenched lawn
in front of the house was a rich,
startling green. I could hear the swish
of traffic on Division Street.
I was nineteen, bereft and lonely.
When I woke, I was sixty-nine.

Gratitude Ahead

I wake early. The cats know
my pattern and after racing me
to the living room, sit primly,
waiting for their special treat,
their calm green eyes
observing me. I fill
their water bowl
while the kettle heats
water for my tea,
top off the kibble,
do a little clean-up.
The water is hot.
I measure the herbal mixture
into my cup, open the blinds
to the winter morning—
pale yellow sky,
bare branches,
patches of snow
on the ground.
My friend tells me
to thank ahead.
"That's what we do,"
she assures me.
She is a big Mohawk woman
and knowledgeable
of certain ways. So
I begin my morning prayers
thanking Creator
for the good care
about to come my way,

for the thoughtful offers of aid
that will arrive from friends,
for my sisters' visits
next month,
and the month after,
and after that. I must
thank ahead for recovery,
for restoration, my strength
returning little by little.
Gratitude ahead
for Creator's love
that persists,
who knows why, when
we humans could do
so much better?
I thank ahead for light,
the shimmering vibration
of daybreak casting its glow
upon our urban yards
and alleys, engulfing
every stark corner, illuminating
dark casements and dormers.
I love this hour when night retreats
to the west, but not before
greeting the first faint rays,
as I do, watching
from my kitchen window.

Evening

When daylight fades behind the mountains,
deer emerge from shadows, stepping lightly
through the falling dusk. They pause
alert and wary, and watch as humans pass.
Their eyes glisten, they sniff the air, then
resume their gentle pace, following a path
laid down long ago. Thus a lean doe
leads her young to safety
among thick willows
that grow by the culvert,
or they'll bed down under the scraggly elms
and cottonwoods that line the old ditch.
Meanwhile, thin stars, faintly glowing,
appear in the deepening sky.
Towards midnight they will flare
like torches, lighting our path upwards.

Midnight

In this soft hour I am most alone
searching my heart for poetry.
I write these words in secret,
stumbling through vocabularies
and over vowel sounds,
the hard consonants
of worry and despair,
asking myself for truth.
One day we will leave
this whirling planet, blue
and precious like a child's marble.
Must we abandon our mother?
Wake up, dear soul. Let's walk
in the night garden
where the upturned earth
smells of loam, where flowers
laden with scent open
among the mint
and small strawberries.
Let's look to the mountain
where we can discern a dusting of snow
beneath the moon's reflected light,
listen to the trickle of water
in the fountain, feel the last of today's heat
lift from the paving stones.
Were we not invited to love this place
with tenderness and respect?
Were we not formed with the very dirt
we will have to one day bid farewell—
fragrant soil made of stardust

and rain? Let's walk in the garden
and feel the night wind on our faces.
Give me your warm hand to kiss.

Kiss

We were in the blue pickup,
giddy from wine,
conversation,
and poetry. Earlier
we had roamed the shelves
of a bookstore. *Do you
know this book? What about
this?* It was late,
we were on Broadway
in that northwest town.
I had pulled over to the curb
to let you out, and now
came the moment
to say farewell, *adiós,*
till next time. We were
smiling at each other,
laughing, when suddenly
your lips grazed my cheek.
I turned and kissed you
too, a funny smooch
like I give the grandkid.
Then quietly, one more,
lingering slightly, wondering
without words, *What
does it mean?* We parted,
that's all I know,
going separate ways,
but for awhile
the imprint of your kiss
remained.

Ahimsa

You ask me, *What is your aim?*
Ahimsa, says my soul. Yet
to live a peaceful life
is no easy thing. Each moment
we must find our balance
on this revolving sphere
that seems so solid
beneath our feet.
Each moment
as we breathe the air,
we come closer
to dying,
or watching others die,
and it seems every thought
contains the potential
to harm another,
to disappoint, betray,
indulge in elaborate
dishonesty, the flaw
of human character.
Find the darkest room,
you tell me, *and fasten on*
the small and steady glimmer
of the morning star. She greets you
as a friend. I understand.
It's quiet. I can hear
the soft drum of my pulse,
the high whistle of melody
in my ear, the meander of
my own dark thoughts.

Sometimes tears well up
and rush in hot streams
down my face. Sometimes
I sweat my human sweat,
salty and pungent, though I'm alone
in this cold room. I despair
of the violent hurricanes
that trample so many lives—
fish in the ocean, coral reefs,
animals, mothers mourning
the loss of their children.
I bring to my lips the sweet
word *ahimsa,* the incredible word
truth. *They exist,* you tell me,
in the here and now,
in this place of sorrow.
I tread this path with care.

Poetry

What is your aim? she asks.
Poetry, I answer with the tongue
of my thought. *Find the first word,*
she tells me, *and go from there.*
She is smiling at me
lovingly, so I believe her.

Integrity

How can you be a poet?
my mother asks. *You can't*
even read a poem with
any understanding.
True. Poetry baffles me.
I struggle to make sense—
if that is what it is—
of its metaphors,
images, symbols,
and all the rest of
that difficult *patois*.
But here I am in my teens
imagining there must be
a future, a grown-up life
where I have something
called "a career" and
where I walk upright
instead of crawling along
in my shell, my eyes
goggling orbs, trying
to discover my path.
With that question
I am almost splayed
on the roadway, this brittle
encumbrance that protects me
almost crushed
by heavy footfall. I don't know
why I want to be a poet.
Perhaps because I need
a language for

the knowledge
I have been accumulating
lately, words that shine
with the slow, steady glimmer
of my heart. I believe
in its integrity, though
I have not yet reached
a way to say this
aloud. If only I could
thread my way through
the eye of that needle—
poetry—I could begin to stitch
the pieces together
into a coherent garment.
Mom laughs. *You couldn't even*
put together an A-line skirt!
If I hadn't finished that project for you,
you would have failed your sewing class.
True. I hate sewing.

Chimayó

Much is closed down in this town,
not just boarded up, but
crumbling to dust—houses,
stores, sheds, barns—
going back to sand,
pink and pale brown,
the color of my skin.
Massive cottonwoods
abound, thick-barked,
their grey limbs askew,
leafy greenness turning yellow
in the wind. Still the apples ripen,
crisp and red, and a burro brays
in his pasture beneath the trees.
September days are mild
now the sun is moving south,
its fierce persistence dimmed.
Down the road another mile
the little sanctuary stands
where believers come
for a cup of holy dirt
one can dig with a spoon
from the loamy floor,
a soil that heals, miraculous
as light. I realize now
that I'm no good
without my glass of wine
and bit of bread at night,
the voice of my beloved
in my ear, telling me

her day—tasks completed, those
left to do, thoughts
that got away, plans
gone astray. What comfort I find
when I contemplate my friend.
I'm attached. I loathe
to turn my back
on this ball of matter,
hard-packed and continuously
breaking down. I want
to sit here on the patio
this breezy day and sing
praise for all I love—here
in this overgrown garden
where cherry boughs welcome
small birds, below the hill
where horses stamp the clay
and water churns along
the acequia's rough
trough. Today I can accept
how winter comes
with mist and snow and fog.

Daybreak

Already traffic has begun to pass,
one car after another in this
busy lifetime, chasing, fleeing,
being pursued, cruising a highway
thick with dreams. Contours of hills
and the bright chamisa grow distinct,
begin to shimmer in the first light,
first chill, first growl of the belly.
A rooster crows. First breeze
begins to blow, stirring the willow's
stringy branches, lifting dust devils
in the dry creek bed. The dead,
perched on roadside crosses,
watch benignly, contemplating
the faces of the living, set
so grimly on the task
of moving forward. Each day
the chapel bell will ring,
calling the faithful to prayer
and collectors of refuse
will spring awake, full of coffee,
ready to drive the big
unwieldy trucks, empty
except for discarded
accumulations. What kind
of fear is this that paces the quiet
rooms of this abode, that waits
for daybreak so that it might sleep
again? What kind of desire
keeps me at this job

or any other, what kind of sorrow,
what kind of lust? Daybreak
and the chipper birds are winging
south. A few stray clouds
have gathered over the mountains
but will be gone by noon,
dispersed by warming air,
unknowable,
irretrievable.

St. Faith

There's another pilgrim on the road,
shuffling through the gravel,
brushing up against the sunflowers,
walking stick or crutch in hand,
making his way to Our Lady
with her blue, star-filled cape,
the spikes of her corona
wavering in warm air
around her dark head
bent in fastidious prayer.
The pilgrim is about to ask
permission, for he needs
the aid of that small boy
whom he knows was once himself
in guaraches and a floppy hat,
still innocent and helpful,
wandering the alleys of his town
before the brutal world
broke in and made him—
in his words—*very bad.*
Perhaps the solicitous mom
will intercede. And so we find him
on the road. Unlike the fancy folk,
he's come adorned with faith,
or at least with hope,
t-shirt torn, pants bagging
at the knees. He comes
unshaven, or unshorn,
headband shadowed with sweat,
mornings or afternoons,

when the creased and crenellated
cliffs around here glow
with a kind of radiance,
and heavy trees seem arched
in sympathy, their crown of leaves
turned gold from shortened days
and colder nights. And now
the pilgrim stops to ask the way,
then stumbles on with hot
and swollen feet. And now
the purple clouds of sunset
spread their wings and fly,
besotted angels, across the pale
evening sky, heading south,
before sharply turning east
toward *Tsi Mayoh*.

Sunday

I like to stand in the doorway
and contemplate the hills
behind Santa Fe, the foot,
I'm told, of the Rockies,
the massive chain of peaks
that arrange themselves
northward from here.
They come to a halt
quite humbly at this end
in soft, rounded shapes
with wooded slopes and crests.
Indians in these parts
named some hills sacred,
know them as the birthplace
of certain holy ones,
beings of power that provide
insight about living right:
how to be generous, forgive,
seek wisdom, have courage,
nurture life, face death.
Remind the spirit to connect
with Creator—a thin word
for an eternal force
that has no name,
or perhaps names itself
beyond our comprehension.
We humans feel compelled
to put words to everything
we touch, sense, or feel,
to every thought,

even those thoughts
that lie below language,
unspoken, without sound.
Like the hills that were
touched by Creator's hand,
and so are holy. They remain
mutely at attention, paying heed
to something longer lasting
than the here and now. I guess
it's why we meditate, why
we pray, make music,
poetry, dance—the arts
and art that keeps trying
to nudge our memory,
keep us humble, warn us
against greed, arrogance,
selfishness, sloth—all the oafish
things that make us real,
yet rob us of our chance
to be human.

Beloved

Driving north from Albuquerque, I watch
the land open up: wide river plains
dried out, awash with sage
and yellow-tufted chamisa,
white cliffs beleaguered by wind,
red banks of earth that form
high, flat-topped mesas,
and farther off, gray mountains
cresting the remnants of an old volcano.
Clouds build and thicken in blue sky,
but withhold the rain, or if it falls,
it evaporates in parched air
before reaching this desiccated,
beautiful earth. Why am I in love?
Why this dark affection?
Why this awe and this lament?
I try to find a melody
that would match my longing,
my grief, my tender appreciation—
all the moments I hurt her,
or that she, knowingly or not,
marred me, negligent of my fealty
and my fierce regard: did she know
of my despair? No sin this adoration
of matter—bones, flesh, hair,
blood—but pain ever turning
from the source of this flesh, this flame,
this fury.

Night

I want to be where I can see the stars,
in the darkest hours of the day,
when everything's gone still:
clouds slip beyond the ridge and
drift away, wind ceases fingering
the fragrant sage, my restless heart
stops prowling through its hungers.
I love the mystery of light
that comes here from afar—
silver, teal, or white—always there,
even if we go about our hours unaware
of that bright glittering. Night
spreads her black hair across
the pillow of the universe.
She yields and appeases, tasting
of pomegranate, scented like musk.
Night is this listening, this quiet
meditation, the pain of ardor
quelled, when you and I find ourselves
untethered, afloat in dreams—
where spirit draws nourishment
from the icy, astral stream,
and returns us, kindly,
to our own steaming breath.

Day

Day's exuberance begins. I am a student
opening a lucid text, curious
to learn its strange sounds,
its exalted lexicon. Here is
a map to pore over,
the pronunciation key,
a discoverable grammar,
lists of untold words
about to be uttered
into my first hearing, like
a prayer in Latin, a song
in French or Portuguese,
*chanson et fleur, um fado
inconsolável.* Day breaks
with crow squawks,
screech of jays, the *wha-wha-
wha-wha* of the nuthatch
exploring the linden tree,
and morning brightens,
ebullient even with fog hovering
or a little rain—so much
the better. I have emerged
from dark into the waking dawn,
into the *what ifs,*
the *yeses,* the world of
possibility sputtering along
like a little Vespa. Wind,
fresh from the sea, is
in my hair, on my face.
I greet everything!

Eventide

Old cat napping near me on the sofa
as I work this eventide. Tremor
of paw as she drops into sleep,
a deep sigh. Day has closed down,
the sky purple-hued, color
of violets, and finally, now
it's dusk, a cooling in the air.
Summer's turned to fall:
dry grass, ripened squash,
pumpkins grown dense
with seeds and pulp. All this
wild and viney florescence
poking its way through
the wooden fence, busting
the broken slats, covering
moistened earth in a corner
of our garden. Soon the moon
will rise in the somber sky,
yellow and heavy-looking
as the thick gourds
in the neighbor's yard.
Soon I'll hear the old cat's
purring snore, the small cries
she makes in her sleep, rhythmic
noises of contentment
and relief, now I'm home
where I ought to be—or so
she made it clear to me
after I'd been gone
a month. Eventide

and dinner's done,
dishes soaking in the sink,
I'm working till night
falls complete
and the cold sets in.
I'm working till sleep
forces me to bed,
where I'll lie, curled
as a fern frond
around a dream,
emitting soft meows,
my paws twitching.

Simple

I am a simple woman.
I rise early, drink coffee,
feed the cats. Satisfied,
they find places to nap
while I sit on the sofa
and wait, staring at nothing
until through some small
persistence, I am able to tap
a few words here
on a page. See?
Simple. I wait
some more: quiet
enjoyment. *Perhaps*
if I crack open
the window of my heart,
I think, *I will hear again*
the little bell that chimed
five times, a tone precise
and mysterious. It came
through thin air,
a morning much like this.
It came in a moment
of prayer or meditation.
Perhaps I was on my knees,
eyes closed, ears open,
the usual buzz going on—
mind chatter—then *ping,*
ping, ping, ping,
ping—it stopped me.
Everything was listening—

tall redwoods in the backyard,
jay on the neighbor's lawn,
even the wavering glass
in the window rested,
attuned to the vibration.
Funny how ordinary
it was, that gentle tone
entering my room
from nowhere, though
perhaps it was ever there,
waiting for me. Like pure memory
it was an honest sound, clean
and round. It faded
in the customary way,
so I got up, went downstairs
musing and amused. Life
was going on—Mom sewing,
dogs scratching themselves,
a cat asleep on the laundry.
Outside the window, leaves
on the ornamental plum
fluttered—everything
as simple as always.

Meditation

Father, remember how we walked
cool mornings in spring
on the dirt road
east of the university?
Venus might be setting
in the pale sky, glowing
lamp-like above the white city
that rose at the edge
of the blue-black bay.
Many times we stood
observing the same scene,
no words spoken, so I could not
know your thoughts, nor
did you ask for mine.
Perhaps in your mind
you reassured me, or maybe,
instead, you begged me
to understand the pain
you thought I might feel too—
its sharpness honed by years
of secrecy and evasion. But then
you'd whistle for the dogs,
a reedy sound, thin
and high,
and we'd start home,
where surely disappointment
lingered, the daily fare
of argument, belittlement,
aggravation. Still,
what pleasure to be greeted

by that one small, creamy
iris opened in the yard, revealing
its pale blue tongue.

Contradiction

Rebellious I am called
whenever I scowl,
energetic fists pounding walls,
one foot smashing the door.
Insanity, they say.
The girl's crazy.
I am sane enough,
but utterly constrained.
Tough, that's what I want
to be in jeans
and blue work shirts,
my cropped hair tousled
by the wind.
Next to prissy girls,
I am a tomboy,
running hard,
crossing boundaries
of decorum,
envious of freedom,
wanting to shape my own.
Inwardly I know myself
to be night, full of shadows,
moon-sick. Easy
to follow the heart
into forests, snowfields,
to gaze at the frozen creek
or ice-edged pastures
where horses graze.
Silence is my name
when I stand, tantalized

by another girl's grace,
ardent, pretending
I do not see. No reaching
across that chasm.
Clearly a sin
that never feels wrong
except when I am found out.

Snow

Snow is falling
this hushed winter day.
It slants like rain,
but looks thicker.
Gusts of wind knock it
from the linden's black branches
and it spirals upwards
before falling decidedly
towards earth.
What can I tell you
about snow?
If you were to stand
in the snow
and lift your face
to its touch,
it would melt
on your cheeks and eyelids.
But soon you would assimilate
to its presence, becoming whiter
and more frigid.
Icicles would form
on your brows, in your hair,
in your nostrils.
Breathing snow is agony.
But I remember snowfalls
when I was a child
and we lived briefly
in Idaho beneath tall,
dark pines and the coarse snow
came, drifting mutely,

covering the gravelly hill,
down to the frozen shores
of the lake. We might stomp
our way to the little store,
crossing the wooden footbridge
over the icy creek where
stark willows stood. (This
was long before I had a notion
about my wrongness,
which if I knew it, I kept
to myself, for my dreams
were certainly strange
and could not be revealed).

And much later, when snowfalls
came and went all winter in Oregon
where I lived apart from my family
and fell in love,
my friends and I smoked cigarettes
rather than eating, and watched
the snow cover the lawn,
the steps, the balustrade.
And wasn't that a lonely time,
each of us unable to say
what we feared, having learned
almost no language
for that particular alarming feeling,
so large and smothering?
(But was it not enticing
to find another
who warmly accepted
your kisses, who
pressed herself to you late

at night in the dim room
among the shadows?)
(And did you not both
remain silent about
the vulnerable passion that
absorbed you? Did you not stare
in mute confusion when her lover
visited and she was paired—just
as it should be—and you
could not protest?)

(And was she not hurt by you,
and did she not do things to herself
that hurt her more? And
didn't you see her weeks later,
crouched over in the overheated ward
with industrial yellow walls
and pipes that kept clanging with steam?
Didn't her father arrive
in that interstice between storms
when clouds sat very low
on the hills and the river moved
slowly, so quiet—you knew this,
though you would not notice
till later you walked across the bridge—
and then she was gone?)
Oh, snow, snow, snow.
What can I tell you
about snow that
you do not already
understand?

Mrs. Ryder's Hands

I'd met them in the cannery,
Mrs. Ryder,
and her middle daughter,
Patsy, a blond with a chortling laugh
and swinging hips. Engaged
to an Air Force guy, Patsy
told common jokes
that shocked,
but other times amused me.

September passed,
and I hung out with them.
When it turned early Fall
they invited me to Lyle
where they lived,
across the river. I went
with them after work
in their old Studebaker.

Outside their white frame house
stood a line of cedars
that blocked the north wind.
It was a cozy place,
an old farmhouse
with an oil-burning heater
and a new T.V.
in a fake wood cabinet.

The first couple of weekends,
Patsy and I did the only things

it seemed there were to do:
had coke at the bowling alley
in White Salmon,
and rode horses
on the tableland
above the Columbia River.

They gave me Patsy's room
when I visited while she slept
in the cottage next to the house
that had been her grandma's quarters.

The room had a sloping ceiling
and a small window
that looked out
on a nearby Douglas fir
and the long pasture.
From her bed, I could see
fading yellow grass, a dark
lapis sky, the wooded
hills of Oregon.

When I stayed with the Ryders,
I got up early,
had my coffee, chatted
with Patsy's father
who drove equipment
in a road crew. He told me
about hunting deer
in eastern Oregon,
and how some city slickers
would shoot wild burros,
not knowing the difference.

One Sunday at their place
I woke up to a blustery morning:
rain, low clouds, and wind
twisting the cedars.
Mrs. Ryder had gotten out
a plastic pan and was making bread
in the warm kitchen. No one else
was awake.

It was peaceful drinking coffee,
watching her sift the flour
and start the dough. Her hands
reminded me of my mom's,
soft, but capable and hard-working.

She turned and kneaded the dough,
rolling it over, pushing it
with her knuckles.
I'd seen my mom do this
many times. I remembered
the way my mother
shoved her hair
with the back of her wrist,
as this woman did.

Suddenly I ached, wishing
I could see my mom again,
though we seldom got along.

Mrs. Ryder punched the dough
a final time. She sighed,
turned the pocked

and yeasty brain,
pushed it with both fists.

"It disgusts me," she began,
"that you want to kiss my girl.
I've seen how you watch her
and believe me, if I ever
catch you in the same bed,
you'll never set foot
in this house again."

She paused and
looked at me directly.
"Do you understand?"

My heart crumbled.
I stared at her hands,
too dumb to blink.

Fierce Defense

See, I love my daughters, those
three beautiful girls. I'd kill any s.o.b.
who tried to hurt them. This is
why that morning you sat with me
in the kitchen, I said something.
You'd been spending time with us,
eating at our table in the company cafeteria,
running out with Patsy and the other
cannery girls before the one o'clock whistle,
lounging with them on the grassy slope
by the library.
Patsy told me—and I saw—
how quiet you were, how she tried
to make you laugh. She told those silly
jokes, but you hardly cracked a smile.
I could see you were sad about something.
You aren't unfriendly, only
shy. You look at Patsy
with adoring eyes, which she loves.
She is a flirt, I admit, but
it comes so natural to her
she's unaware of her effect.

She never meant for you
to fall for her. Girls can't
love other girls. Not really.
Not the way a man can love.
The good Lord made us this way
on purpose. But I started to suspect
when I heard some of those songs

you sing, playing your guitar—
pretty ballads, words about cheating
hearts and lying tongues. I got
worried. You don't talk. You
sing your desires. I knew
I had to put a stop to it,
even if it hurt you.

Because, after all, you are not
one of mine. And I will not have
my daughter turned lesbian
by the likes of you, a half-breed
who comes from California. Folks
smoke dope there and
engage in free love.

Love, they call it. That's not
what love is. I will tell you
what it is—this searing
pain when you imagine anything
bad happening to your kids.
When you've labored to bring a life
into this world, and you struggle
to shape that life, you can't let
some stranger come and
mess with it. No.

I'd heard of your kind
having fights outside seedy bars
with their girl lovers, man-hating
so-and-so's who have to live
furtive and sly.
                    When I looked up

from my work, I saw you crying, out
by the cedar trees. The rain
had let up, but if it were pouring
you'd be in it, trying to
wash away my words,
which I spoke from the truth
in my heart. Maybe you were
lonely and sad, but that
is not my affair. If you want
to be a queer, that is not
my business either.
But don't come around my door
with those ideas, don't try
to influence my daughter.

My girl is young, susceptible
to many things, but that's one way
of being that I will never
give way to, never
tolerate.

Black Hair

You should always do
what you want to do, she says,
stooping to check
a side of elk
roasting in the oven.
So I step forward
and touch her hair,
which is long and black
and shining. She freezes
mid-crouch and looks up at me,
startled. I step away,
heart beating hard.
Is she angry?
Beyond a doubt
she must know
my longing, but
she says nothing,
just straightens,
closes the oven's door
and strides to the table
where she sits, crosses her legs,
and pulls a long cigarette
from an almost full pack.
The children are asleep
on the living room floor,
since the one bedroom
of that small house
is occupied by her
and her husband
who is, I suppose,

away hunting. Do I sleep
on the sofa that night,
or does she invite me
to share her bed?
I don't remember,
but it seems to me next morning
she's up early, making coffee.
My job starts at seven
and the factory is
at least an hour's drive
along the two-lane highway
that borders the swollen river.
Snow has fallen all night
in the black hours before dawn,
blanketing the narrow road
outside her place, piling up
beneath the trees. She's awake
to prepare a sandwich for me—
slices of elk steak on thick,
homemade bread,
which she wraps
in waxed paper.
She fills my thermos.
Neither of us say much.
What's to say?
She watches me eat
the egg she's fried for me,
and the smell of tobacco
mingles with the scent
of breakfast and coffee.
She's pinned her black hair
in a wispy chignon.
Her youngest child

crawls out of a sleeping bag
and moves sleepily towards her,
rubbing an eye, barely awake.
She scoops the girl,
sets her gently on her lap
and nuzzles the child's hair.
I pull on my pea coat,
and trudge out to start my car,
knock snow from the windshield
with a broom, sweep it
with a woolen sleeve.
I go back in the house
to thank her, to gather
my guitar, my belongings,
the lunch bucket.
Drive carefully, she says.
The child is nestled
in her arms. I nod an answer.
On the highway logging trucks
roar by me on the way to the mill.
Snow tumbles down fast,
spiraling out of the sky.
I drive, staring hard at the dark.
Do I regret caressing her hair?
I contemplate how she stood
in the warm kitchen, wrapping
that hearty sandwich.

Today

I find it hard to be
among the living—
squabbles, quarrels,
people wound up
like tops, tight, then
flung, spinning
sideways, coming
to a wobbly stop
on hot pavement.
I much prefer the dead
or the imagined,
the vivid ontology of myth
to the story of history:
griffins, dragons,
horses with wings.
The Little People
and Small Deer
of the Cherokee,
inhabiting forests
and meadows scented
with sweetgrass.
If I could only stay
here in the faint
stare of my eyes,
fingers to lips, body
barely moving except
in this exhaling
that heaves through
heavy atmosphere. Oh,
breath instead of tears,

lament, this tilted world,
stilted and hurt.
There is too much
of everything,
and not enough
of anything: bread,
water, trees. Sweet music,
they say, surges
among planets and stars.
For me it's inaudible.

Benediction

Our indigenous earth breathes
lightly at dawntime,
watching the sky.
She greets the sun,
nodding slowly
at the slender light—
Beauty above me—
She observes the fiery residue
stars leave as they trail westward,
the southward winging
of geese and cranes.
In narrow marshes,
a faint breeze
stirs the cat-tails,
a pair of barn owls
return to roost
in the rafters
of an old shed,
the sora wakes
and begins to peck
and poke among the reeds.
To be alone is all she wants,
gathering herself inwardly
as darkness wanes. *Beauty*
below me—Listening
to surrounding stillness,
she notices stones at rest
after their nightly journey.
Cold arrives, tree roots
dig down, burrowing

toward earth's center,
the gravity of existence
returning like a memory.
Rainclouds roll in and rivers
turn somnolent, purple asters
pale in high valleys,
a whisper of mountain snow
settles quietly
among the crags,
on north-facing slopes.
Beauty behind me, beauty
before me—her first thought
and last. It spirals out
in all directions,
like happiness.

Visitations

1.
Above us the blue sky
of summer and a slight mist
drifting at the edge of hills,
threading among the spruce
and pines, overlooking the sea
and the long, narrow bay.

After lunch we hike
beneath those trees, among
the toyon and manzanita
that line the trail. Below us
we can see a shelf of land that curves
into a cove, above which gulls are circling.
Some stand one-legged on the warm sand,
looking about with yellow eyes.

What year is it? What Saturday
or Sunday picnic is this?
Is Mom still able to walk
in her usual brisk manner,
or has that cold visitor arrived
to sit at one end of the outdoor table,
dressed in ordinary black, gazing
at the far water, saying nothing
while tapping his fingers lightly
on the checkered cloth?

My jacket is suede, deep green
with brass buttons. My mother's coat

soft gray. These are the skins
we wear today. We pose for
a picture together, one
that Daddy snaps. We smile,
holding aloft our cheese and crackers.
A crow eyes us from a stump.
Other birds thrash among the seaside
shrubs, chattering. I decide
that Mom is weary.
The chemo has depleted her.
The cells have resumed
their crazy replication,
and this takes energy too.

2.
Why can we never see his face?
It is always averted, in shadow.
He looks down, he looks away,
but he never looks directly
at us. He must realize
he causes immense pain,
but he carries out his duties
like a mission, a necessity
even in the most horrific
or untidy circumstances.
Like a rescue.

3.
I know nothing about the soul.
I perceive the green hills fading to yellow
all summer long, fog rolling down
among the pines, billowing in waves,
much like the surf, but quiet,

leaving a trace in the steady drip
of condensation that falls
to earth, soaking the roadside
grass, the brambles of blackberries
choking ravines. From some bog
or marsh, a great blue heron rises,
pushing upward against the air
with strong wings. I think a soul
might rise that way too. It might
struggle up against the downward pull
of rocks, stones, and roots, might
rise into the lighter atmosphere
high above the fog, the clouds,
the far blue. It might dissolve.

4.
Years later I want to forgive
my parents for lapses, flaws,
lacerations, neglects. Love
isn't perfect. I look for ways
to make it right. Usually
that means a table, cleared of
newspapers, tools, books,
set meticulously with the great brown
or white cloth, tall candles,
the Azulejo vase filled
with freesias from the corner market.
Then plates of food, the pasta and bread,
a bowl of salad, cool wine
in our sturdy glasses.
Someone has repurposed
the clear Christmas lights.
They frame the curve of the dining room

window that looks out on the old garden.
That is where I stand, year after year.
The calla lilies have spiraled open
and the Leopard lily. The frilly
dark magenta petals of the Sweet Williams,
Mom's favorite flower, surprise us:
Who planted them? When?

5.
He came down the stairs, Mom said,
the man in black, recalling the first time
she had ever seen him.
He said nothing,
made no noise.
He must have walked out
through the front door.
Next day came the telegram:
her brother had died.

They had been sitting at the table.
It was made of oak
in the Mission style.
Mom's three adoptive mothers
sat with her, talking primly.
She was still a child,
or perhaps a young teen.
She looked up
to see him pass
and asked, *Who was that?*
But no one else had noticed.

6.
If they take me up to Idaho

when I die, and bury me next to Ivan,
said Aunt Lillian, *my spirit will*
just get up and come right back
to California.

It was too hot to be inside
where a chicken was roasting
for Saturday supper.
We sat on lawn chairs—Mom,
Aunty, my sister, and me—
beneath the elms. I could hear
the clack-clack-clack of a sprinkler,
could smell cut alfalfa from nearby fields
as simmering heat began to rise
from the valley floor.

Aunt Lillian got up from her chair
and stood looking around at us
with nearly sightless eyes.
She wore her "mule mouth,"
as Mom called it, a stubborn
expression, hard and adamant.

Mom nodded, said nothing. We all knew
her soul would find a way.

7.
I like this drift of memories
and spend a lot of time here,
driving to Pt. Reyes
and back home to Berkeley,
rain or sun, fog or wind.
Thermoses of tea, coffee

or cocoa empty, someone
hands around sections
of a peeled orange,
or a package of cookies. Funny
how the journey home
invites contemplation
rather than conversation,
everyone watching the highway,
the woods, clouds passing
over the crest of hills, horses
in pastures, stalks of dry thistle.

Funny to remember the place
along this road I picked up
three girls hitchhiking,
the place my car broke down
and Dad had to come for me,
the hillside where the prickly pear
cactus grows wild, the old movie theater,
a back road up Tamalpais,
the 1930s houses, tile-roofed,
painted white, some architect's
dream of Mexico or Spain.
Then the long span of bridge
over the silver-bright water,
smell of refineries,
oil tankers at dock,
the dark east bay hills
gray-green in the afternoon
light. And finally
the winding streets
of our town, pungent
smell of eucalyptus,

heavy shadows,
the chilly north slope
where our house sits
among redwoods
and rhododendron.

I know so little
about the soul. But I think
we are always heading homeward,
determined to arrive,
finally welcomed.

Beyond Knowing

If I look with the corners
of my eyes to that place
where poetry begins,
images may appear, despite
the ringing in my ears
and raging in my mind,
the imperious demands
of what they call the future,
or furious denunciations
of self. Looking
is the beginning
of seeing, the risk one takes
in discerning what is there:
rattlesnake coiled
by the roadside, history
buried under abandoned
foundations, the stain of blood
on quilts and blankets.
If I look with the right eye,
I see my own intention
extending into the distance
past the place where
the earth curves
into a light blue sky.
If I look with the left eye,
I settle into my own breath,
feel the beat of an invisible heart,
the tremor of soul fastened
to the integuments of my body.
If I look beyond

the corners of knowing,
I can see the shimmer
of a different light,
illuminating what could be
naked, small truths—
ocean-washed agates
along the north coast,
spider's web bedecked
with spatters of dew,
even a discarded cat's claw,
shining on the hardwood floor.

Notes

The quote from Marilou Awaikta's *Selu: Seeking The Corn-Mother's Wisdom* opens the first paragraph of the chapter titled "Daydreaming Primal Space: Cherokee Aesthetics as Habits of Being."

In the poem "St. Faith," p. 28, the images are of the Virgin of Guadalupe and the Santo Niño de Atocha, familiar figures in Catholic New Mexico. Especially at Easter, but at other times as well, one sees pilgrims, some of them on crutches, en route to the Sanctuario de Chimayó, where they hope to be healed of infirmities. Tsi Mayoh is the Tewa name for this place the sanctuary occupies.

"Mrs. Ryder's Hands," p.46, was translated into French as "Les mains de Mme Ryder" by Béatrice Machet. This poem and "Fierce Defense" were published in an anthology of Native American women's poetry, *De l'autre côté du chagrin: Anthologie de poetesses Indiennes*. "Fierce Defense," p.50, was translated as "Défense féroce." The anthology was published by Editions Wallâda in 2018.

Headmistress Press Books

Seed - Janice Gould

The Princess of Pain - Carolyn Gage & Sudie Rakusin

She/Her/Hers - Amy Lauren

Spoiled Meat - Nicole Santalucia

Cake - Jen Rouse

The Salt and the Song - Virginia Petrucci

mad girl's crush tweet - summer jade leavitt

Saturn coming out of its Retrograde - Briana Roldan

i am this girl - gina marie bernard

Week/End - Sarah Duncan

My Girl's Green Jacket - Mary Meriam

Nuts in Nutland - Mary Meriam, Hannah Barrett

Lovely - Lesléa Newman

Teeth & Teeth - Robin Reagler

How Distant the City - Freesia McKee

Shopgirls - Marissa Higgins

Riddle - Diane Fortney

When She Woke She Was an Open Field - Hilary Brown

God With Us - Amy Lauren

A Crown of Violets - Renée Vivien tr. Samantha Pious

Fireworks in the Graveyard - Joy Ladin

Social Dance - Carolyn Boll

The Force of Gratitude - Janice Gould

Spine - Sarah Caulfield

I Wore the Only Garden I've Ever Grown - Kathryn Leland

Diatribe from the Library - Farrell Greenwald Brenner

Blind Girl Grunt - Constance Merritt

Acid and Tender - Jen Rouse

Beautiful Machinery - Wendy DeGroat

Odd Mercy - Gail Thomas

The Great Scissor Hunt - Jessica K. Hylton

A Bracelet of Honeybees - Lynn Strongin

Whirlwind @ Lesbos - Risa Denenberg

The Body's Alphabet - Ann Tweedy

First name Barbie last name Doll - Maureen Bocka

Heaven to Me - Abe Louise Young

Sticky - Carter Steinmann

Tiger Laughs When You Push - Ruth Lehrer

Night Ringing - Laura Foley

Paper Cranes - Dinah Dietrich

On Loving a Saudi Girl - Carina Yun

The Burn Poems - Lynn Strongin

I Carry My Mother - Lesléa Newman

Distant Music - Joan Annsfire

The Awful Suicidal Swans - Flower Conroy

Joy Street - Laura Foley

Chiaroscuro Kisses - G.L. Morrison

The Lillian Trilogy - Mary Meriam

Lady of the Moon - Amy Lowell, Lillian Faderman, Mary Meriam

Irresistible Sonnets - ed. Mary Meriam

Lavender Review - ed. Mary Meriam

www.ingramcontent.com/pod-product-compliance
Lightning Source LLC
Chambersburg PA
CBHW071237090426
42736CB00014B/3119